Informing the legislative debate since 1914 _____

Multiyear Procurement (MYP) and Block Buy Contracting in Defense Acquisition: Background and Issues for Congress

Ronald O'Rourke
Specialist in Naval Affairs

Moshe Schwartz
Specialist in Defense Acquisition

June 25, 2014

Congressional Research Service

7-5700

www.crs.gov

R41909

Summary

Multiyear procurement (MYP) and block buy contracting (BBC) are special contracting mechanisms that Congress permits the Department of Defense (DOD) to use for a limited number of defense acquisition programs. Compared to the standard or default approach of annual contracting, MYP and BBC have the potential for reducing weapon procurement costs by several percent.

Under annual contracting, DOD uses one or more contracts for each year's worth of procurement of a given kind of item. Under MYP, DOD instead uses a single contract for two to five years' worth of procurement of a given kind of item without having to exercise a contract option for each year after the first year. DOD needs congressional approval for each use of MYP. There is a permanent statute governing MYP contracting—10 U.S.C. 2306b. Under this statute, a program must meet several criteria to qualify for MYP.

Compared with estimated costs under annual contracting, estimated savings for programs being proposed for MYP have ranged from less than 5% to more than 15%, depending on the particulars of the program in question, with many estimates falling in the range of 5% to 10%. In practice, actual savings from using MYP rather than annual contracting can be difficult to observe or verify because of cost growth during the execution of the contract due to changes in the program independent of the use of MYP rather than annual contracting.

BBC is similar to MYP in that it permits DOD to use a single contract for more than one year's worth of procurement of a given kind of item without having to exercise a contract option for each year after the first year. BBC is also similar to MYP in that DOD needs congressional approval for each use of BBC. BBC differs from MYP in the following ways:

- There is no permanent statute governing the use of BBC.

- There is no requirement that BBC be approved in both a DOD appropriations act and an act other than a DOD appropriations act.

- Programs being considered for BBC do not need to meet any legal criteria to qualify for BBC, because there is no permanent statute governing the use of BBC that establishes such criteria.

- A BBC contract can cover more than five years of planned procurements.

- Economic order quantity (EOQ) authority—the authority to bring forward selected key components of the items to be procured under the contract and purchase the components in batch form during the first year or two of the contract—does not come automatically as part of BBC authority because there is no permanent statute governing the use of BBC that includes EOQ authority as an automatic feature.

- BBC contracts are less likely to include cancellation penalties.

Potential issues for Congress concerning MYP and BBC include whether to use MYP and BBC in the future more frequently, less frequently, or about as frequently as they are currently used; and whether to create a permanent statute to govern the use of BBC, analogous to the permanent statute that governs the use of MYP.

Contents

Tables

Appendixes

Contacts

Introduction

Issues for Congress

This report provides background information and issues for Congress on multiyear procurement (MYP) and block buy contracting (BBC),[1] which are special contracting mechanisms that Congress permits the Department of Defense (DOD) to use for a limited number of defense acquisition programs. Compared to the standard or default approach of annual contracting, MYP and BBC have the potential for reducing weapon procurement costs by several percent.

Potential issues for Congress concerning MYP and BBC include whether to use MYP and BBC in the future more frequently, less frequently, or about as frequently as they are currently used; and whether to create a permanent statute to govern the use of BBC, analogous to the permanent statute (10 U.S.C. 2306b) that governs the use of MYP. Congress's decisions on these issues could affect defense acquisition practices, defense funding requirements, and the defense industrial base.

Terminology and Scope of Report

Two Air Force "Block Buys" That Are Not Discussed in This Report

Evolved Expendable Launch Vehicle (EELV) Launch Services (ELS) Contract

A contract that the Air Force has for the procurement of Evolved Expendable Launch Vehicle (EELV) Launch Services (ELS) is sometimes referred to as a block buy, but it is not an example of block buy contracting as discussed in this report. The Air Force in this instance is using the term block buy to mean something different. This report does not discuss the ELS contract.

Procurement of Two AEHF Satellites

For FY2015, the Air Force is requesting continued procurement funding for two Advanced Extremely High Frequency (AEHF) satellites that were procured in FY2012 and partially funded in FY2012-FY2014. Although the Air Force refers to this two-satellite procurement as a block buy, it is not an example of block buy contracting as discussed in this report. The Air Force in this instance is using the term block buy to mean something different. For further discussion, see "Terminology Alert: Block Buy Contracting vs. Block Buys" below.

Funding Approaches vs. Contracting Mechanisms

In discussing MYP and BBC, it can be helpful to distinguish funding approaches from contracting mechanisms. The two are often mixed together in discussions of DOD acquisition, sometimes leading to confusion. Stated briefly:

---

[1] MYP is an established acronym for multiyear procurement. BBC is not an established acronym for block buy contracting, but is used in this CRS report for purposes of convenience.

- **Funding approaches** are ways that Congress can appropriate funding for weapon procurement programs, so that DOD can then put them under contract. Examples of funding approaches include traditional full funding (the standard or default approach), incremental funding, and advance appropriations.[2] Any of these funding approaches might make use of advance procurement (AP) funding.[3]

- **Contracting mechanisms** are ways for DOD to contract for the procurement of weapons systems, once funding for those systems has been appropriated by Congress. Examples of contracting mechanisms include annual contracting (the standard or default approach), MYP, and BBC.

The use of a particular funding approach in a defense acquisition program does not dictate the use of a particular contracting mechanism. Defense acquisition programs consequently can be implemented using various combinations of funding approaches and contracting mechanisms. Most DOD weapon acquisition programs use a combination of traditional full funding and annual contracting. A few programs, particularly certain Navy shipbuilding programs, use incremental funding as their funding approach. A limited number of DOD programs use MYP as their contracting approach, and to date at least two defense acquisition programs (both Navy shipbuilding programs) use or have used BBC as their contracting approach.

This report focuses on the contracting approaches of MYP and BBC and how they compare to annual contracting. Other CRS reports discuss the funding approaches of traditional full funding, incremental funding, and advance appropriations.[4]

Background

Multiyear Procurement (MYP)

MYP in Brief

What is MYP, and how does it differ from annual contracting? MYP, also known as multiyear contracting, is an alternative to the standard or default DOD approach of annual contracting.

---

[2] For more on these three funding approaches, see CRS Report RL31404, *Defense Procurement: Full Funding Policy— Background, Issues, and Options for Congress*, by Ronald O'Rourke and Stephen Daggett, and CRS Report RL32776, *Navy Ship Procurement: Alternative Funding Approaches—Background and Options for Congress*, by Ronald O'Rourke. Advance appropriations, which are not to be confused with advance procurement (AP) funding (see footnote 3), are essentially a legislatively locked-in form of incremental funding. Unlike incremental funding, advance appropriations qualify under budgeting regulations as a form of full funding.

[3] AP funding is provided in one or more years prior to the year of procurement of a weapon system for the procurement of long-leadtime components—components with long construction times. Such components must be funded prior to the procurement of the remainder of the weapon system if they are to be ready for installation in the weapon system at the appropriate point in the construction process. AP funding is a permitted exception to the full funding provision. AP funding is not to be confused with advance appropriations (see footnote 2).

[4] See footnote 2 for citations to these reports. Appropriating funding for a program and placing a program under contract are steps in a larger sequence of budget-related events that includes authorization, appropriation, obligation, and outlays. For a general discussion of this sequence, see CRS Report 98-721, *Introduction to the Federal Budget Process*, coordinated by Bill Heniff Jr.

Under annual contracting, DOD uses one or more contracts for each year's worth of procurement of a given kind of item. Under MYP, DOD instead uses a single contract for two to five years' worth of procurement of a given kind of item, without having to exercise a contract option for each year after the first year. DOD needs congressional approval for each use of MYP.

To illustrate the basic difference between MYP and annual contracting, consider a hypothetical DOD program to procure 20 single-engine aircraft of a certain kind over the five-year period FY2015-FY2019, at a rate of four aircraft per year:

- **Under annual contracting**, DOD would issue one or more contracts for each year's procurement of four aircraft. After Congress funds the procurement of the first four aircraft in FY2015, DOD would issue one or more contracts (or exercise a contract option) for those four aircraft. The next year, after Congress funds the procurement of the next four aircraft in FY2015, DOD would issue one or more contracts (or exercise a contract option) for those four aircraft, and so on.

- **Under MYP**, DOD would issue one contract covering all 20 aircraft to be procured during the five-year period FY2015-FY2019. DOD would award this contract in FY2015, at the beginning of the five-year period, following congressional approval to use MYP for the program, and congressional appropriation of the FY2015 funding for the program. To continue the implementation of the contract over the next four years, DOD would request the FY2016 funding for the program as part of DOD's proposed FY2016 budget, the FY2017 funding as part of DOD's proposed FY2017 budget, and so on.

Potential Savings Under MYP

How much can MYP save? Compared with estimated costs under annual contracting, estimated savings for programs being proposed for MYP have ranged from less than 5% to more than 15%, depending on the particulars of the program in question, with many estimates falling in the range of 5% to 10%. In practice, actual savings from using MYP rather than annual contracting can be difficult to observe or verify because of cost growth during the execution of the contract that was caused by developments independent of the use of MYP rather than annual contracting.

A February 2012 briefing by the Cost Assessment and Program Evaluation (CAPE) office within the Office of the Secretary of Defense (OSD) states that "MYP savings analysis is difficult due to the lack of actual costs on the alternative acquisition path, i.e., the path not taken."[5] The briefing states that CAPE up to that point had assessed MYP savings for four aircraft procurement programs—F/A-18E/F strike fighters, H-60 helicopters, V-22 tilt-rotor aircraft, and CH-47F helicopters—and that CAPE's assessed savings ranged from 2% to 8%.[6]

A 2008 Government Accountability Office (GAO) report stated that

---

[5] Slide 10 from briefing entitled "Multiyear Procurement: A CAPE Perspective," given at DOD cost analysis symposium, February 15-17, 2012, posted at InsideDefense.com (subscription required) May 14, 2012.

[6] Slide 12 from briefing entitled "Multiyear Procurement: A CAPE Perspective," given at DOD cost analysis symposium, February 15-17, 2012, posted at InsideDefense.com (subscription required) May 14, 2012. Slide 12 also stated that these assessed savings were based on comparing CAPE's estimate of what the programs would cost under annual contracting (which the briefing refers to as single-year procurement or SYP) to the contractor's MYP proposal.

DOD does not have a formal mechanism for tracking multiyear results against original expectations and makes few efforts to validate whether actual savings were achieved by multiyear procurement. It does not maintain comprehensive central records and historical information that could be used to enhance oversight and knowledge about multiyear performance to inform and improve future multiyear procurement (MYP) candidates. DOD and defense research centers officials said it is difficult to assess results because of the lack of historical information on multiyear contracts, comparable annual costs, and the dynamic acquisition environment.[7]

How does MYP potentially save money? Compared to annual contracting, using MYP can in principle reduce the cost of the weapons being procured in two primary ways:

- **Contractor optimization of workforce and production facilities.** An MYP contract gives the contractor (e.g., an airplane manufacturer or shipbuilder) confidence that a multiyear stream of business of a known volume will very likely materialize. This confidence can permit the contractor to make investments in the firm's workforce and production facilities that are intended to optimize the facility for the production of the items being procured under the contract. Such investments can include payments for retaining or training workers, or for building, expanding, or modernizing production facilities. Under annual contracting, the manufacturer might not have enough confidence about its future stream of business to make these kinds of investments, or might be unable to convince its parent firm to finance them.

- **Economic order quantity (EOQ) purchases of selected long-leadtime components.** Under an MYP contract, DOD is permitted to bring forward selected key components of the items to be procured under the contract and to purchase the components in batch form during the first year or two of the contract. In the hypothetical example introduced earlier, using MYP could permit DOD to purchase, say, the 20 engines for the 20 aircraft in the first year or two of the five-year contract. Procuring selected components in this manner under an MYP contract is called an economic order quantity (EOQ) purchase.[8] EOQ purchases can reduce the procurement cost of the weapons being procured under the MYP contract by allowing the manufacturers of components to take maximum advantage of production economies of scale that are possible with batch orders.[9]

---

[7] Government Accountability Office, *Defense Acquisitions[:] DOD's Practices and Processes for Multiyear Procurement Should Be Improved*, GAO-08-298, February 2008, p. 3.

[8] The term EOQ is occasionally used in discussions of defense acquisition, somewhat loosely, to refer to any high-quantity or batch order of items, even those that do not take place under MYP or BBC. As a general matter, however, EOQs as described here occur only within MYP and block buy contracts.

[9] A 2008 Government Accountability Office (GAO) report on multiyear contracting lists five areas of savings, most of which are covered in the two general areas of savings outlined above. One of GAO's five areas of savings—limited engineering changes due to design stability—can also occur in programs that use annual contracting. The GAO report states:

> Multiyear procurement can potentially save money and improve the defense industrial base by permitting the more efficient use of a contractor's resources. Multiyear contracts are expected to achieve lower unit costs compared to annual contracts through one or more of the following sources: (1) purchase of parts and materials in economic order quantities (EOQ), (2) improved production processes and efficiencies, (3) better utilized industrial facilities, (4) limited engineering changes due to design stability during the multiyear period, and (5) cost avoidance by reducing the

(continued...)

What gives the contractor confidence that the multiyear stream of business will materialize? At least two things give the contractor confidence that DOD will not terminate an MYP contract and that the multiyear stream of business consequently will materialize:

- For a program to qualify for MYP, DOD must certify, among other things, that the minimum need for the items to be purchased is expected to remain substantially unchanged during the contract in terms of production rate, procurement rate, and total quantities.

- Perhaps more important to the contractor, MYP contracts include a cancellation penalty intended to reimburse a contractor for costs that the contractor has incurred (i.e., investments the contractor has made) in anticipation of the work covered under the MYP contract. The undesirability of paying a cancellation penalty acts as a disincentive for the government against canceling the contract. (And if the contract is canceled, the cancellation penalty helps to make the contractor whole.)[10]

Permanent Statute Governing MYP

Is there a permanent statute governing MYP contracting? There is a permanent statute governing MYP contracting—10 U.S.C. 2306b. The statute was created by Section 909 of the FY1982 Department of Defense Authorization Act (S. 815/P.L. 97-86 of December 1, 1981), revised and reorganized by Section 1022 of the Federal Acquisition Streamlining Act of 1994 (S. 1587/P.L. 103-355 of October 13, 1994), and further amended on several occasions since. DOD's use of MYP contracting is further governed by DOD acquisition regulations.

Under this statute, what criteria must a program meet to qualify for MYP? 10 U.S.C. 2306b(a) states that to qualify for MYP, a program must meet several criteria, including the following.

- **Substantial savings.** DOD must estimate that using an MYP contract would result in "substantial savings" compared with using annual contracting.

- **Realistic cost estimates.** DOD's estimates of the cost of the MYP contract and the anticipated savings must be realistic.

- **Stable need for the items.** DOD must expect that its minimum need for the items will remain substantially unchanged during the contract in terms of production rate, procurement rate, and total quantities.

(...continued)

> burden of placing and administering annual contracts. Multiyear procurement also offers opportunities to enhance the industrial base by providing defense contractors a longer and more stable time horizon for planning and investing in production and by attracting subcontractors, vendors, and suppliers. However, multiyear procurement also entails certain risks that must be balanced against potential benefits, such as the increased costs to the government should the multiyear contract be changed or canceled and decreased annual budget flexibility for the program and across DOD's portfolio of weapon systems. Additionally, multiyear contracts often require greater budgetary authority in the earlier years of the procurement to economically buy parts and materials for multiple years of production than under a series of annual buys.

Government Accountability Office, *Defense Acquisitions[:] DOD's Practices and Processes for Multiyear Procurement Should Be Improved*, GAO-08-298, February 2008, pp. 4-5.

[10] Annual contracts can also include cancellation penalties.

- **Stable design for the items.** The design for the items to be acquired must be stable, and the technical risks associated with the items must not be excessive.

Section 811 of the FY2008 National Defense Authorization Act (H.R. 4986/P.L. 110-181 of January 28, 2008) amended 10 U.S.C. 2306b to require the Secretary of Defense to certify in writing, by no later than March 1 of the year in which DOD requests MYP authority for a program, that these and certain other criteria have been met. It also requires that the Secretary provide the congressional defense committees with the basis for this determination, as well as a cost analysis performed by DOD's office of Cost Assessment and Program Evaluation (CAPE) that supports the findings.[11] Section 811 further amended 10 U.S.C. 2306b to require the following:

- **Sufficient prior deliveries to determine whether estimated unit costs are realistic.** A sufficient number of the type of item to be acquired under the proposed MYP contract must have been delivered under previous contracts at or within the most current estimates of the program acquisition unit cost or procurement unit cost to determine whether current estimates of such unit costs are realistic.

- **No Nunn-McCurdy critical cost growth breaches within the last five years.** The system being proposed for an MYP contract must not have experienced within five years of the anticipated award date of the MYP contract a critical cost growth breach as defined under the Nunn-McCurdy act (10 U.S.C. 2433).[12]

- **Fixed-price type contract.** The proposed MYP contract must be a fixed-price type contract.

What is meant by "substantial savings"? The meaning of "substantial savings" is open to interpretation and might depend on the circumstances of the program in question. In practice, estimated savings of at least 5% might be judged substantial, and estimated savings in the range of 10% (or more) are more likely to be judged substantial. The amount of savings required under 10 U.S.C. 2306b to qualify has changed over time; the requirement for "substantial savings" was established by Section 808(a)(2) of the FY1991 National Defense Authorization Act (H.R. 4739/P.L. 101-510 of November 5, 1990), which amended 10 U.S.C. 2306b in this regard.[13]

What is meant by "stable design"? The term "stable design" is generally understood to mean that the design for the items to be procured is not expected to change substantially during the period of the contract. Having a stable design is generally demonstrated by having already built at least a few items to that design (or in the case of a shipbuilding program, at least one ship to that design) and concluding, through testing and operation of those items, that the design does not require any substantial changes during the period of the contract.

---

[11] §811 states that the cost analysis is to be performed by DOD's Cost Analysis Improvement Group (CAIG). In a subsequent DOD reorganization, CAIG was made part of CAPE.

[12] For more on the Nunn-McCurdy provision, see CRS Report R41293, *The Nunn-McCurdy Act: Background, Analysis, and Issues for Congress*, by Moshe Schwartz.

[13] For a discussion of the evolution of the savings requirement under 10 U.S.C. 2306b, including a figure graphically summarizing the legislative history of the requirement, see Government Accountability Office, *Defense Acquisitions[:] DOD's Practices and Processes for Multiyear Procurement Should Be Improved*, GAO-08-298, February 2008, pp. 21-22, including Figure 3 on p. 22.

Potential Consequences of Not Fully Funding an MYP Contract

What happens if Congress does not provide the annual funding requested by DOD to continue the implementation of the contract? If Congress does not provide the funding requested by DOD to continue the implementation of an MYP contract, DOD would be required to renegotiate, suspend, or terminate the contract. Terminating the contract could require the government to pay a cancellation penalty to the contractor. Renegotiating or suspending the contract could also have a financial impact.

Effect on Flexibility for Making Procurement Changes

What effect does using MYP have on flexibility for making procurement changes? A principal potential disadvantage of using MYP is that it can reduce Congress's and DOD's flexibility for making changes (especially reductions) in procurement programs in future years in response to changing strategic or budgetary circumstances, at least without incurring cancellation penalties. In general, the greater the portion of DOD's procurement account that is executed under MYP contracts, the greater the potential loss of flexibility. The use of MYP for executing some portion of the DOD procurement account means that if policy makers in future years decide to reduce procurement spending below previously planned levels, the spending reduction might fall more heavily on procurement programs that do not use MYP, which in turn might result in a less-than-optimally balanced DOD procurement effort.

Congressional Approval

How does Congress approve the use of MYP? Congress approves the use of MYP on a case-by-case basis, typically in response to requests by DOD.[14] Congressional approval for MYP contracts with a value of more than $500 million must occur in two places: an annual DOD appropriations act[15] and an act other than the annual DOD appropriations act.[16]

In annual DOD appropriations acts, the provision permitting the use of MYP for one or more defense acquisition programs is typically included in the title containing general provisions, which typically is Title VIII.

An annual defense authorization act is usually the act other than an appropriations act in which provisions granting authority for using MYP contracting on individual defense acquisition programs are included. Such provisions typically occur in Title I of the defense authorization act, the title covering procurement programs.

---

[14] The Anti-Deficiency Act (31 U.S.C. 1341) prohibits the making of contracts in advance of appropriations. A multiple-year commitment may be made when authorized by Congress by entering into a firm commitment for one year and making the government's liability for future years contingent on funds becoming available.

[15] Paragraph (3) of subsection (l) of 10 U.S.C. 2306b states, "The head of an agency may not initiate a multiyear procurement contract for any system (or component thereof) if the value of the multiyear contract would exceed $500,000,000 unless authority for the contract is specifically provided in an appropriations Act."

[16] Paragraph (3) of subsection (i) of 10 U.S.C. 2306b states, "In the case of the Department of Defense, a multiyear contract in an amount equal to or greater than $500,000,000 may not be entered into for any fiscal year under this section unless the contract is specifically authorized by law in an Act other than an appropriations Act."

Provisions in which Congress approves the use of MYP for a particular defense acquisition program may include specific conditions for that program in addition to the requirements and conditions of 10 U.S.C. 2306b.

How often is MYP used? MYP is used for a limited number of DOD acquisition programs. As shown in the **Appendix**, annual DOD appropriations acts since FY1990 typically have approved the use of MYP for one or a few DOD programs each year.

A February 2012 briefing by the Cost Assessment and Program Evaluation (CAPE) office within the Office of the Secretary of Defense (OSD) shows that the total dollar value of DOD MYP contracts has remained more or less stable between FY2000 and FY2012 at roughly $7 billion to $13 billion per year. The briefing shows that since the total size of DOD's procurement budget has increased during this period, the portion of DOD's total procurement budget accounted for by programs using MYP contracts has declined from about 17% in FY2000 to less than 8% in FY2012.[17] The briefing also shows that the Navy makes more use of MYP contracts than does the Army or Air Force, and that the Air Force made very little use of MYP in FY2010-FY2012.[18]

A 2008 Government Accountability Office (GAO) report stated:

> Although DOD had been entering into multiyear contracts on a limited basis prior to the 1980s, the Department of Defense Authorization Act, [for fiscal year] 1982,[19] codified the authority for DOD to procure on a multiyear basis major weapon systems that meet certain criteria. Since that time, DOD has annually submitted various weapon systems as multiyear procurement candidates for congressional authorization. Over the past 25 years, Congress has authorized the use of multiyear procurement for approximately 140 acquisition programs, including some systems approved more than once.[20]

In an interview published on January 13, 2014, Sean Stackley, the Assistant Secretary of the Navy for Research, Development, and Acquisition (i.e., the Navy's acquisition executive), stated:

> What the industrial base clamors for is stability, so they can plan, invest, train their work force. It gives them the ability in working with say, the Street [Wall Street], to better predict their own performance, then meet expectations in the same fashion we try to meet our expectations with the Hill.
>
> It's emblematic of stability that we've got more multiyear programs in the Department of the Navy than the rest of the Department of Defense combined. We've been able to harvest from that significant savings, and that has been key to solving some of our budget problems. It's allowed us in certain cases to put the savings right back into other programs tied to requirements.[21]

---

[17] Slide 4 from briefing entitled "Multiyear Procurement: A CAPE Perspective," given at DOD cost analysis symposium, February 15-17, 2012, posted at InsideDefense.com (subscription required) May 14, 2012.

[18] Slide 5 from briefing entitled "Multiyear Procurement: A CAPE Perspective," given at DOD cost analysis symposium, February 15-17, 2012, posted at InsideDefense.com (subscription required) May 14, 2012.

[19] S. 815/P.L. 97-86 of December 1, 1981, §909.

[20] Government Accountability Office, *Defense Acquisitions[:] DOD's Practices and Processes for Multiyear Procurement Should Be Improved*, GAO-08-298, February 2008, p. 5.

[21] "Interview: Sean Stackley, US Navy's Acquisition Chief," *Defense News*, January 13, 2014: 22.

Block Buy Contracting (BBC)

BBC in Brief

What is BBC, and how does it compare to MYP? BBC is similar to MYP in that it permits DOD to use a single contract for more than one year's worth of procurement of a given kind of item without having to exercise a contract option for each year after the first year.[22] BBC is also similar to MYP in that DOD needs congressional approval for each use of BBC.

BBC differs from MYP in the following ways:

- There is no permanent statute governing the use of BBC.

- There is no requirement that BBC be approved in both a DOD appropriations act and an act other than a DOD appropriations act.

- Programs being considered for BBC do not need to meet any legal criteria to qualify for BBC because there is no permanent statute governing the use of BBC that establishes such criteria.

- A BBC contract can cover more than five years of planned procurements. The BBC contracts currently being used by the Navy for procuring Littoral Combat Ships (LCSs), for example, cover a period of six years (FY2010-FY2015).

- Economic order quantity (EOQ) authority does not come automatically as part of BBC authority because there is no permanent statute governing the use of BBC that includes EOQ authority as an automatic feature. To provide EOQ authority as part of a BBC contract, the provision granting authority for using BBC in a program may need to state explicitly that the authority to use BBC includes the authority to use EOQ.

- BBC contracts are less likely to include cancellation penalties.

Given the one key similarity between BBC and MYP (the use of a single contract for more than one year's worth of procurement), and the various differences between BBC and MYP, BBC might be thought of as a less formal stepchild of MYP.

When and why was BBC invented? BBC was invented by Section 121(b) of the FY1998 National Defense Authorization Act (H.R. 1119/P.L. 105-85 of November 18, 1997), which granted the Navy the authority to use a single contract for the procurement of the first four Virginia (SSN-774) class attack submarines. The four boats were scheduled to be procured during the five-year period FY1998-FY2002 in annual quantities of 1-1-0-1-1. Congress provided the authority granted in Section 121(b) at least in part to reduce the combined procurement cost of the four submarines. Using MYP was not an option for the Virginia-class program at that time

---

[22] Using the hypothetical example introduced earlier involving the procurement of 20 aircraft over the five-year period FY2013-FY2017, DOD would follow the same general path as it would under MYP: DOD would issue one contract covering all 20 aircraft in FY2013, at the beginning of the five-year period, following congressional approval to use BBC for the program, and congressional appropriation of the FY2013 funding for the program. To continue the implementation of the contract over the next four years, DOD would request the FY2014 funding for the program as part of DOD's proposed FY2014 budget, the FY2015 funding as part of DOD's proposed FY2015 budget, and so on.

because the Navy had not even begun, let alone finished, construction of the first Virginia-class submarine, and consequently could not demonstrate that it had a stable design for the program.

When Section 121(b) was enacted, there was no name for the contracting authority it provided. The term block buy contracting came into use later, when observers needed a term to refer to the kind of contracting authority that Congress authorized in Section 121(b). As discussed in the next section, this can cause confusion, because the term block buy was already being used in discussions of DOD acquisition to refer to something else.

Terminology Alert: Block Buy Contracting vs. Block Buys

What's the difference between block buy contacting and block buys? In discussions of defense procurement, the term "block buy" by itself (without "contracting" at the end) is sometimes used to refer to something quite different from block buy contracting—namely, the simple act of funding the procurement of more than one copy of an item in a single year, particularly when no more than one item of that kind might normally be funded in a single year. For example, when Congress funded the procurement of two aircraft carriers in FY1983, and another two in FY1988, these acts were each referred to as block buys, because aircraft carriers are normally procured one at a time, several years apart from one another. This alternate meaning of the term block buy predates by many years the emergence of the term block buy contracting.

The term block buy is still used in this alternate manner, which can lead to confusion in discussions of defense procurement. For example, for FY2014, the Air Force is requesting continued procurement funding for two Advanced Extremely High Frequency (AEHF) satellites that were procured in FY2012 and partially funded in FY2012 and FY2013. (An alternative approach would have been to procure one of the satellites in FY2012 and another in a subsequent year.) The Air Force is referring to this two-satellite procurement as a block buy—which it is, under the older use of the term. But it is not an example of block buy *contracting*.

At the same time, Navy officials sometimes refer to the use of block buy contracts for the first four Virginia-class submarines, and currently in the LCS program, as block buys, when they might be more specifically referred to as instances of block buy *contracting*.

Potential Savings Under BBC

How much can BBC save, compared with MYP? Potential savings under BBC can be less than those under MYP, for at least two reasons:

- The authority to use BBC might not include authority to use EOQ purchasing, which, as discussed earlier (see "Potential Savings Under MYP"), is one of the two principal sources of savings under an MYP contract. The block buy contract for the first four Virginia-class boats and the current block buy contracts for the LCS program do not include authority for EOQ purchasing.

- A BBC contract might not include a cancellation penalty (or might include a more limited one). This can give the contractor less confidence than would be the case under an MYP contract that the future stream of business will materialize as planned, which in turn might reduce the amount of money the contractor invests to optimize its workforce and production facilities for producing the items to be procured under the contract.

Frequency of Use of BBC

How frequently has BBC been used? Since its use at the start of the Virginia-class program, BBC has been used very rarely. The Navy did not use it again in a shipbuilding program until December 2010, when it awarded two block buy contracts, each covering 10 LCSs to be procured over the six-year period FY2010-FY2015, to the two LCS builders.[23]

Using BBC Rather than MYP

When might BBC be suitable as an alternative to MYP? BBC might be particularly suitable as an alternative to MYP in cases where using a multiyear contract can reduce costs, but the program in question cannot meet all the statutory criteria needed to qualify for MYP. As shown in the case of the first four Virginia-class boats, this can occur at or near the start of a procurement program, when design stability has not been demonstrated through the production of at least a few of the items to be procured (or, for a shipbuilding program, at least one ship).

MYP and BBC vs. Contracts with Options

What's the difference between an MYP or block buy contract and a contract with options? The military services sometimes use contracts with options to procure multiple copies of an item that are procured over a period of several years. The Navy, for example, used a contract with options to procure Lewis and Clark (TAKE-1) class dry cargo ships that were procured over a period of several years. A contract with options can be viewed as somewhat similar to an MYP or block buy contract in that a single contract is used to procure several years' worth of procurement of a given kind of item.

There is, however, a key difference between an MYP or block buy contract and a contract with options: In a contract with options, the service is under no obligation to exercise any of the options, and a service can choose to not exercise an option without having to make a penalty payment to the contractor. In contrast, in an MYP or block buy contract, the service is under an obligation to continue implementing the contract beyond the first year, provided that Congress appropriates the necessary funds. If the service chooses to terminate an MYP or block buy contract, and does so as a termination for government convenience rather than as a termination for contractor default, then the contractor can, under the contract's termination for convenience clause, seek a payment from the government for cost incurred for work that is complete or in process at the time of termination, and may include the cost of some of the investments made in anticipation of the MYP or block buy contract being fully implemented. The contractor can do this even if the MYP or block buy contract does not elsewhere include a provision for a cancellation penalty.[24]

---

[23] For further discussion, see CRS Report RL33741, *Navy Littoral Combat Ship (LCS) Program: Background and Issues for Congress*, by Ronald O'Rourke.

[24] Source: Telephone discussion with Elliott Branch, Deputy Assistant Secretary of the Navy for Acquisition & Procurement, October 3, 2011, and email from Navy Office of legislative Affairs, October 11, 2011. Under the termination for convenience clause, the contractor can submit a settlement proposal to the service, which would become the basis for a negotiation between the contractor and the service on the amount of the payment.

Issues for Congress

Potential issues for Congress concerning MYP and BBC include whether to use MYP and BBC in the future more frequently, less frequently, or about as frequently as they are currently used; and whether to create a permanent statute to govern the use of BBC, analogous to the permanent statute that governs the use of MYP.

Frequency of Using MYP and BBC

Should MYP and BBC in the future be used more frequently, less frequently, or about as frequently as they are currently used? Supporters of using MYP and BBC more frequently in the future might argue the following:

- Since MYP and BBC can reduce procurement costs, making greater use of MYP and BBC can help DOD get more value out of its available procurement funding. This can be particularly important if DOD's budget in real (i.e., inflation-adjusted) terms remains flat or declines in coming years, as many observers anticipate.

- The risks of using MYP have been reduced by Section 811 of the FY2008 National Defense Authorization Act (H.R. 4986/P.L. 110-181 of January 28, 2008), which amended 10 U.S.C. 2306b to strengthen the process for ensuring that programs proposed for MYP meet certain criteria (see "Permanent Statute Governing MYP"). Since the value of MYP contracts equated to less than 8% of DOD's procurement budget in FY2012, compared to about 17% of DOD's procurement budget in FY2000, MYP likely could be used more frequently without exceeding past experience regarding the share of DOD's procurement budget accounted for by MYP contracts.

Supporters of using MYP and BBC less frequently in the future, or at least no more frequently than now, might argue the following:

- Using MYP and BBC more frequently would further reduce Congress's and DOD's flexibility for making changes in DOD procurement programs in future years in response to changing strategic or budgetary circumstances. The risks of reducing flexibility in this regard are increased now because of uncertainties in the current strategic environment and because efforts to reduce federal budget deficits could include reducing DOD spending, which could lead to a reassessment of U.S. defense strategy and associated DOD acquisition programs.

- Since actual savings from using MYP and BBC rather than annual contracting can be difficult to observe or verify, it is not clear that the financial benefits of using MYP or BBC more frequently in the future would be worth the resulting further reduction in Congress's and DOD's flexibility for making changes in procurement programs in future years in response to changing strategic or budgetary circumstances.

Permanent Statute for BBC

Should Congress create a permanent statute to govern the use of BBC, analogous to the permanent statute (10 U.S.C. 2306b) that governs the use of MYP? Supporters of creating a permanent statute to govern the use of BBC might argue the following:

- Such a statute could encourage greater use of BBC, and thereby increase savings in DOD procurement programs by giving BBC contracting a formal legal standing and by establishing a clear process for DOD program managers to use in assessing whether their programs might be considered suitable for BBC.

- Such a statute could make BBC more advantageous by including a provision that automatically grants EOQ authority to programs using BBC, as well as provisions establishing qualifying criteria and other conditions intended to reduce the risks of using BBC.

Opponents of creating a permanent statute to govern the use of BBC might argue the following:

- A key advantage of BBC is that it is *not* governed by a permanent statute. The lack of such a statute gives DOD and Congress full flexibility in determining when and how to use BBC for programs that may not qualify for MYP, but for which a multiyear contract of some kind might produce substantial savings.

- Such a statute could encourage DOD program managers to pursue their programs using BBC rather than MYP. This could reduce discipline in DOD multiyear contracting if the qualifying criteria in the BBC statute are less demanding than the qualifying criteria in 10 U.S.C. 2306b.

FY2015 Budget Submission Proposals That Could Affect Existing MYP and BBC Contracts

Navy Littoral Combat Ships (LCSs) in FY2015

As part of its proposed FY2015 budget, the Navy is requesting funding for the procurement of three Littoral Combat Ships (LCSs), rather than four LCSs, as called for under the two LCS block buy contracts, which cover fiscal years FY2010-FY2015 and call two LCSs for each of the two LCS builders in FY2015. If three rather than four LCSs are procured in FY2015, one of the two LCS block buy contracts would not be completely fulfilled in FY2015, the final year of the contract. In testimony this year, the Navy has stated that if three LCSs are funded in FY2015, the Navy will seek to renegotiate one of the two block buy contracts so that the fourth LCS that was previously planned for FY2015 can instead be procured in FY2016.[25]

---

[25] For further discussion, see CRS Report RL33741, *Navy Littoral Combat Ship (LCS) Program: Background and Issues for Congress*, by Ronald O'Rourke.

Navy MH-60R Helicopters in FY2016

The Navy's FY2015 budget submission projects a request for no MH-60R helicopters in FY2016, as opposed to 29 MH-60Rs in FY2016, as called for under two Army-Navy MYP contracts—one for H-60 helicopter air frames, and one for H-60 mission avionics and common cockpit—that cover fiscal years FY2012-FY2016. If no MH-60R helicopters are procured in FY2016, the government would need to terminate these two MYP contracts in their final year. The Chief of Naval Operations testified in March 2014 that the cost of terminating the contracts would be about the same for the Navy as the cost of procuring the aircraft.[26] A subsequent estimate is that the cost to the government would be about $250 million.[27]

An April 9, 2014, press report states:

> Sikorsky Aircraft said on Wednesday [April 9] the U.S. Navy's plan to skip orders for 29 MH-60 helicopters in the final year of a five-year contract could undermine the industry's willingness to sign such cost-saving agreements in the future.
>
> Any move by the Navy to "break" the agreement in fiscal 2016 could also raise the cost of 60 U.S. Army Black Hawk helicopters included in the deal, Tim Healy, director of maritime programs for Sikorsky, a unit of United Technologies Corp, said at the annual Navy League conference.
>
> "This is not a legal issue. This is a confidence issue," Healy said. "If multiyear contracts are negotiated and then not followed through ... industry is back to making year-to-year calculations and investments because you never know when the next year's contract is going to be canceled."
>
> Sikorsky signed an $8.5 billion contract with the Army and Navy in July 2012 to buy 653 Black Hawk and Seahawk helicopters through December 2017, a deal that generated significant discounts given the large size of the order.
>
> Navy Captain Jim Glass, program manager for the H-60 helicopters, told reporters he believed this would be the first time the Pentagon has reneged on a multiyear pact with industry....
>
> Senate Armed Services Committee Chairman Carl Levin last month said the Navy's decision to breach the Sikorsky agreement would trigger termination fees of at least $250 million.
>
> Both Healy and Glass said it was difficult to determine the financial effect, or any termination fees, since it remained unclear how the cuts would be implemented.
>
> But Healy said breaking the multiyear agreement would have other far-reaching consequences for the U.S. Department of Defense's ability to reach such deals in the future.

---

[26] See Lara Seligman, "CNO: Seahawk Buy Tied To CVN-73 Fate, Aircraft Cut Would Yield No Savings," *Inside the Navy*, March 17, 2014; Jen DiMascio and Michael Fabey, "U.S. Navy Truncates Multiyear MH-60R Purchase," *Aerospace Daily & Defense Report*, March 14, 2014: 1-2.

[27] Andrea Shalal, "US Navy's Sikorsky Helicopters Cancellation Would Cost Government $250 mln—Levin," *Reuters.com*, March 27, 2014.

The fiscal 2015 budget preserved the multiyear contract for now, Glass said, and included $107 million in advanced procurement funding to ensure production could begin as planned.[28]

An April 14, 2014, press report states:

> The US Navy, in its fiscal 2015 budget proposal, said it wants to cancel a planned buy of 29 MH-60R Seahawk helicopters in 2016.
>
> The service's reasoning is fairly simple: The Navy is considering retiring the aircraft carrier George Washington due to defense spending cuts. Retiring a carrier means one less carrier air wing—which includes MH-60Rs.
>
> But a major hurdle lies in the helicopter cancellation: The Pentagon signed a multiyear procurement deal with Sikorsky Aircraft and Lockheed Martin—makers of the helicopter—for those 29 machines, meaning the costs associated with terminating the contract could end up being higher than the purchase price, according to Defense Department and industry officials.
>
> The cancellation also could hurt the US Army, which is acquiring UH-60M Black Hawk and HH-60M medical evacuation helicopters through the same multiyear procurement deal.
>
> The Pentagon signed the $8.5 billion deal with Sikorsky for at least 653 helicopters in June 2012. Deliveries run through 2017. The deal included options for 263 more helicopters.
>
> Moreover, it could set a bad precedent that makes contractors wary of inking multiyear procurements, which have saved the Pentagon significant money in acquisition costs over the years.
>
> "The biggest change I think—which is troublesome—is I think this would be the first multiyear in the history of the US government to be broken," said Scott Starrett, vice president of government business development for Sikorsky.[29]

An April 15, 2014, press report stated:

---

[28] Andrea Shalal, "U.S. Navy Move to 'Break' Multiyear Deal Worries Industry—Sikorsky," *Reuters.com*, April 9, 2014. First ellipse as in original. Similarly, a March 12, 2014, press report states:

> The Pentagon has indicated it might have to break its multiyear contract with Sikorsky in 2016 and cease buying more of the Navy's MH-60 Seahawk helicopters.
>
> Obviously, Sikorsky's not happy about this, but it also raises questions about whether companies will continue to trust DoD on multiyear contracts, where lower prices are offered due to the the [sic] built-in promise of a bigger buy.
>
> "The extremely competitive pricing that our customer received on that program was built around specific quantities," Samir Mehta, president of defense systems and services at Sikorsky, said at a luncheon yesterday with reporters. The Pentagon's decision "kind of undermines the confidence in the entire industry associated with multiyears... Something like this could lead us back to the days of single year pricing, which doesn't always offer the best value to the government."
>
> (Kate Brannen with Jonathan Topaz and Austin Wright, "Could Industry Lose Confidence In Multiyear Contracts?" *Politico Pro Defense Morning Defense*, March 12, 2014.)

[29] Marcus Weisgerber, "Industry: Bad Precedent Set if DoD Cancels Multiyear Helo Buy," *DefenseNews.com*, April 14, 2014.

The Pentagon will "look at options" so it does not break a multiyear helicopter contract with Sikorsky and Lockheed Martin that includes about 90 aircraft, a senior US Defense Department official said....

"We obviously don't want to break the multiyear, so we're going to look at options to try not to," Frank Kendall, DoD undersecretary for acquisition, technology and logistics, told Defense News after a speech Tuesday [April 15] at a National Defense Industrial Association conference.

Kendall noted that a decision on the multiyear contract is an issue for DoD's 2016 budget.[30]

An April 22, 2014, press report states:

Lockheed Martin Corp (LMT.N) warned on Tuesday that the U.S. Navy's plan to cancel an order for 29 MH-60 helicopters built by Lockheed and Sikorsky Aircraft would result in large termination fees because they are part of five-year agreements signed in 2012.

Lockheed Chief Financial Officer Bruce Tanner told reporters that work had already begun on cockpits and other equipment for the helicopters, which were to be ordered in fiscal year 2016, and a better option might be to finish building the aircraft and then sell them to allies.

"That would probably be a better deal for the taxpayer than paying close to 100 percent and not getting anything for it," he said. "The cost to terminate partially built helicopters is pretty significant relative to the cost to actually finish those helicopters."

Tanner did not provide details on the size of the expected termination fee if the Navy proceeds with its plan to "break" its five-year contracts with both Lockheed, which integrates the radars, cockpit and other equipment on the helicopters, and Sikorsky, the United Technologies Corp (UTX.N) unit which builds the aircraft....

U.S. Navy officials have said they are working closely with the companies and senior Pentagon leaders to understand the cost of cancelling the final 29 Navy helicopters covered by the agreements, but the process has not yet been completed.[31]

Legislative Activity for FY2015

FY2015 National Defense Authorization Act (H.R. 4435/S. 2410)

House

Section 121 of H.R. 4435 as reported by the House Armed Services Committee (H.Rept. 113-446 of May 13, 2014) provides MYP authority for the procurement of Tomahawk Block IV missiles for the Navy. The report also states that

---

[30] Marcus Weisgerber, "DoD Looking for Ways Not To Break MH-60R Helicopter Deal," *DefenseNews.com*, April 15, 2014.

[31] Andrea Shalal, "Lockheed Says Costly for Pentagon If It Cancels MH-60 Helicopters," *Reuters.com*, April 22, 2014.

... the committee applauds the Army for its efforts to accelerate the Engineering Change Proposal (ECP) programs for the M1 Abrams tank, Bradley fighting vehicle and Stryker combat vehicle. The out-year funding reflected in the budget request for fiscal year 2015 indicates a commitment by the Army to move forward with the next major technology upgrades for the existing fleet of weapons systems that would ensure fielding of the highest quality combat vehicles to a smaller force and also sustain the fragile industrial base. However, the committee remains concerned about the stability of Army modernization funding in fiscal year 2016 and beyond given the implications of sequestration. The committee believes multiyear procurement contracts may reduce overall cost and help stabilize the industrial base and notes that there is precedent for successful Army combat vehicle multiyear procurements. Therefore, the committee encourages the Secretary of the Army, in accordance with section 2306b of title 10, United States Code, to request multiyear procurement authority in future budget requests for the Abrams ECP 1, Bradley ECP 2, and Stryker ECP 1 programs. (Page 15)

Regarding Standard Missile 3 (SM-3) Block IB missiles for the Navy, the report states:

The committee supports the funding requested in the budget submission for Advanced Procurement to support long-lead time requirements for these missiles. The committee also supports the likely request in the fiscal year 2016 budget request for multiyear procurement authority for these missile interceptors. The committee believes that a successful negotiation between the Missile Defense Agency and its contractors could drive down the per unit cost of these interceptors and increase the available quantities to the warfighter. (Page 312)

Senate

Section 821 of S. 2410 as reported by the Senate Armed Services Committee (S.Rept. 113-176 of June 2, 2014) states:

SEC. 821. RESTATEMENT AND REVISION OF REQUIREMENTS APPLICABLE TO MULTIYEAR DEFENSE ACQUISITIONS TO BE SPECIFICALLY AUTHORIZED BY LAW.

(a) In General- Subsection (i) of section 2306b of title 10, United States Code, is amended to read as follows:

`(i) Defense Acquisitions Specifically Authorized by Law- (1) In the case of the Department of Defense, a multiyear contract in amount equal to or greater than $500,000,000 may not be entered into under this section unless the contract is specifically authorized by law in an Act other than an appropriations Act.

`(2) In submitting a request for a specific authorization by law to carry out a defense acquisition program using multiyear contract authority under this section, the Secretary shall include in the request a report containing preliminary findings of the agency head required in paragraphs (1) through (6) of subsection (a) together with the basis for such findings.

`(3) A multiyear contract may not be entered into under this section for a defense acquisition program that has been specifically authorized by law to be carried out using multiyear contract authority unless the Secretary of Defense certifies in writing, not later than 30 days before entry into the contract, that each of the following conditions is satisfied:

`(A) The Secretary has determined that each of the requirements in paragraphs (1) through (6) of subsection (a) will be met by such contract and has provided the basis for such determination to the congressional defense committees.

`(B) The Secretary's determination under subparagraph (A) was made after the completion of a cost analysis performed by the Director of Cost Assessment and Program Analysis and such analysis supports the findings.

`(C) The system being acquired pursuant to such contract has not been determined to have experienced cost growth in excess of the critical cost growth threshold pursuant to section 2433(d) of this title within 5 years prior to the date the Secretary anticipates such contract (or a contract for advance procurement entered into consistent with the authorization for such contract) will be awarded.

`(D) A sufficient number of end items of the system being acquired under such contract have been delivered at or within the most current estimates of the program acquisition unit cost or procurement unit cost for such system to determine that current estimates of such unit costs are realistic.

`(E) During the fiscal year in which such contract is to be awarded, sufficient funds will be available to perform the contract in such fiscal year, and the future-years defense program for such fiscal year will include the funding required to execute the program without cancellation.

`(F) The contract is a fixed price type contract.

`(G) The proposed multiyear contract provides for production at not less than minimum economic rates given the existing tooling and facilities.

`(4) If for any fiscal year a multiyear contract to be entered into under this section is authorized by law for a particular procurement program and that authorization is subject to certain conditions established by law (including a condition as to cost savings to be achieved under the multiyear contract in comparison to specified other contracts) and if it appears (after negotiations with contractors) that such savings cannot be achieved, but that substantial savings could nevertheless be achieved through the use of a multiyear contract rather than specified other contracts, the President may submit to Congress a request for relief from the specified cost savings that must be achieved through multiyear contracting for that program. Any such request by the President shall include details about the request for a multiyear contract, including details about the negotiated contract terms and conditions.

`(5)(A) The Secretary may obligate funds for procurement of an end item under a multiyear contract for the purchase of property only for procurement of a complete and usable end item.

`(B) The Secretary may obligate funds appropriated for any fiscal year for advance procurement under a contract for the purchase of property only for the procurement of those long-lead items necessary in order to meet a planned delivery schedule for complete major end items that are programmed under the contract to be acquired with funds appropriated for a subsequent fiscal year (including an economic order quantity of such long-lead items when authorized by law).

`(6) The Secretary may make the certification under paragraph (3) notwithstanding the fact that one or more of the conditions of such certification are not met, if the Secretary determines that, due to exceptional circumstances, proceeding with a multiyear contract under this section is in the best interest of the Department of Defense and the Secretary provides the basis for such determination with the certification.

`(7) The Secretary may not delegate the authority to make the certification under paragraph (3) or the determination under paragraph (6) to an official below the level of Under Secretary of Defense for Acquisition, Technology, and Logistics.'.

(b) Conforming Amendment- Subsection (a)(7) of such section is amended by striking `subparagraphs (C) through (F) of paragraph (1) of subsection (i)' and inserting `subparagraphs (C) through (F) of subsection (i)(3)'.

(c) Effective Date- The amendments made by this section shall take effect on the date of the enactment of this Act, and shall apply with respect to requests for specific authorization by law to carry out defense acquisition programs using multiyear contract authority that are made on or after that date.

Regarding Section 821, S.Rept. 113-176 states:

Restatement and revision of requirements applicable to multiyear defense acquisitions to be specifically authorized by law (sec. 821)

The committee recommends a provision that would clarify and reorganize the reporting and certification requirements of the Department of Defense when requesting specific authorization for multiyear contract authority.

Section 2306b of title 10, United States Code, requires the Secretary of Defense, in the case of a contract equal to or greater than $500.0 million, to certify that certain requirements will be met by the proposed contract no later than March 1st of the year in which the legislative authority to enter into such contract is requested. The Secretary must send a notification of the findings regarding the same requirements 30 days before award of the contract.

The committee finds value in both the certification and the notification, but believes that the timing is reversed. The recommended provision would reorganize the timeline so the Secretary provides the initial findings of the enumerated requirements when requesting multiyear contract authority and then certifies the completed findings prior to contract award.

The committee believes this will provide more reasonable and complete information. (Page 143)

S.Rept. 113-176 also states:

MH–60R helicopters

The budget request included $933.9 million to buy 29 MH–60R helicopters and $106.7 million in advance procurement. The last future years defense program (FYDP) indicated that the Navy intended to buy 29 MH–60R helicopters in fiscal year 2016 to fulfill the Navy's part of the last year of the Army's H–60 multiyear procurement contract. The latest FYDP projects that the Navy will not buy any MH–60R helicopters in fiscal year 2016. Absent action to revise the fiscal year 2016 plan for the Navy, or to apply additional resources to the Army procurement effort, this action by the Navy would cause a government default on the multiyear contract.

The Navy has planned to budget $250.0 million in fiscal year 2016 to cover termination charges. However, the Navy cannot assure the committee that this amount will cover all of the Navy's early termination charges, nor have Navy officials been able to specify what additional costs will fall on the Army if the Navy were to fail to buy the 29 helicopters as planned. At a minimum, the Army would be forced to renegotiate the contract, which will probably delay deliveries and most certainly increase unit costs.

The committee urges the Navy to reconsider this plan during the development of the fiscal year 2016 budget. If the Navy decides to opt out of the multiyear contract next year, the committee expects the Secretary of the Navy to explain how this aircraft reduction is related to the Navy's ship force structure and whether the Navy will be able to meet its requirements with a smaller number of MH–60R helicopters in the future. In the meantime, the committee directs the Secretary of Defense, in consultation with the Secretary of the Army and the Secretary of the Navy, to develop a better estimate of the likely effects if the Navy were to withdraw from the Army's H–60 multiyear procurement contract in fiscal year 2016. The Secretary of Defense should provide that analysis to the congressional defense committees within 90 days. (Page 30)

FY2015 DOD Appropriations Act (H.R. 4870)

House

Section 8010 of H.R. 4870 as reported by the House Appropriations Committee (H.Rept. 113-473 of June 13, 2014) states:

> Sec. 8010. None of the funds provided in this Act shall be available to initiate: (1) a multiyear contract that employs economic order quantity procurement in excess of $20,000,000 in any one year of the contract or that includes an unfunded contingent liability in excess of $20,000,000; or (2) a contract for advance procurement leading to a multiyear contract that employs economic order quantity procurement in excess of $20,000,000 in any one year, unless the congressional defense committees have been notified at least 30 days in advance of the proposed contract award: Provided, That no part of any appropriation contained in this Act shall be available to initiate a multiyear contract for which the economic order quantity advance procurement is not funded at least to the limits of the Government's liability: Provided further, That no part of any appropriation contained in this Act shall be available to initiate multiyear procurement contracts for any systems or component thereof if the value of the multiyear contract would exceed $500,000,000 unless specifically provided in this Act: Provided further, That no multiyear procurement contract can be terminated without 10-day prior notification to the congressional defense committees: Provided further, That the execution of multiyear authority shall require the use of a present value analysis to determine lowest cost compared to an annual procurement: Provided further, That none of the funds provided in this Act may be used for a multiyear contract executed after the date of the enactment of this Act unless in the case of any such contract--

> (1) the Secretary of Defense has submitted to Congress a budget request for full funding of units to be procured through the contract and, in the case of a contract for procurement of aircraft, that includes, for any aircraft unit to be procured through the contract for which procurement funds are requested in that budget request for production beyond advance procurement activities in the fiscal year covered by the budget, full funding of procurement of such unit in that fiscal year;

> (2) cancellation provisions in the contract do not include consideration of recurring manufacturing costs of the contractor associated with the production of unfunded units to be delivered under the contract;

> (3) the contract provides that payments to the contractor under the contract shall not be made in advance of incurred costs on funded units; and

(4) the contract does not provide for a price adjustment based on a failure to award a follow-on contract.

H.Rept. 113-473 states:

MH–60R

The Navy proposes to prematurely terminate the MH–60R helicopter production line in fiscal year 2016, despite the program being bound under a multi-year procurement contract, along with the Army's UH–60 Blackhawk helicopters. The rationale for this termination is due to force structure changes, partially driven by the decision to decrease the number of carrier air wings as a result of the Navy's decision to prematurely decommission the USS George Washington (CVN–73). As discussed elsewhere in this report, the Committee provides the required fiscal year 2015 funding to retain CVN–73, thus obviating that variable as a reason to prematurely terminate the MH–60R procurement program. The Committee directs the Secretary of the Navy to fully fund the remaining MH–60R helicopters as previously planned and fulfill the terms of the joint H–60 multi-year procurement with the Army. (Page 153)

Appendix. Programs Approved for MYP in Annual DOD Appropriations Acts Since FY1990

Table A-1. Programs Approved for MYP in Annual DOD Appropriations Acts Since FY1990

Fiscal Year	Bill/Law	Section on MYP	Program(s) Approved for MYP
2014	H.R. 3547/P.L. 113-76	Section 8010 of Division C	E-2D Advanced Hawkeye
			SSN 774 Virginia class submarine
			KC-130J, C-130J, HC-130J, MC-130J, AC-130J aircraft, and government-furnished equipment
2013	H.R. 933/P.L. 113-6	Section 8010 of Division C	F/A-18E, F/A-18F, and EA-18G aircraft
			Up to 10 DDG-51 destroyers, as well as the AEGIS Weapon Systems, MK 41 Vertical Launching Systems, and Commercial Broadband Satellite Systems associated with those ships
			Virginia class submarines and government-furnished equipment
			CH-47 Chinook helicopters
			V-22 Osprey aircraft variants
2012	H.R. 2055/P.L. 112-74	Section 8010 of Division A	UH–60M/HH–60M and MH–60R/MH–60S Helicopter Airframes
			MH–60R/S Mission Avionics and Common Cockpits
2011	H.R. 1473/P.L. 112-10	Section 8010 of Division A	Navy MH-60R/S helicopter systems
2010	H.R. 3326/P.L. 111-118	Section 8011 of Division A	F-18 aircraft variants
2009	H.R. 2638/P.L. 110-329	Section 8011 of Division C	SSN Virginia class submarine
2008	H.R. 3222/P.L. 110-116	Section 8010 of Division A	Army CH-47 Chinook helicopter
			M1A2 Abrams System Enhancement Package upgrades
			M2A3/M3A3 Bradley upgrades
			SSN Virginia Class submarine
2007	H.R. 5631/P.L. 109-289	Section 8008 of Division A	C-17 Globemaster
			F-22A
			MH-60R Helicopters
			MH-60R Helicopter mission equipment
			V-22 Osprey
2006	H.R. 2863/P.L. 109-148	Section 8008 of Division A	UH-60/MH-60 helicopters
			C-17 Globemaster
			Apache Block II Conversion
			Modernized Target Acquisition Designation Sight/Pilot Night Vision Sensor (MTADS/PNVS)

Fiscal Year	Bill/Law	Section on MYP	Program(s) Approved for MYP
2005	H.R. 4613/P.L. 108-287	Section 8008	Lightweight 155mm Howitzer
2004	H.R. 2658/P.L. 108-87	Section 8008	F/A-18 aircraft
			E-2C aircraft
			Tactical Tomahawk missile
			Virginia Class submarine
2003	H.R. 5010/P.L. 107-248	Section 8008	C-130 aircraft
			FMTV
			F/A-18E and F engine
2002	H.R. 3338/P.L. 107-117	Section 8008 of Division A	UH-60/CH-60 aircraft
			C-17
			F/A-18E and F engine
2001	H.R. 4576/P.L. 106-259	Section 8008	Javelin missile
			M2A3 Bradley fighting vehicle
			DDG-51 destroyer
			UH-60/CH-60 aircraft
2000	H.R. 2561/P.L. 106-79	Section 8008	Longbow Apache helicopter
			Javelin missile
			Abrams M1A2 Upgrade
			F/A-18E/F aircraft
			C-17 aircraft
			F-16 aircraft
1999	H.R. 4103/P.L. 105-262	Section 8008	E-2C aircraft
			Longbow Hellfire missile
			Medium Tactical Vehicle Replacement (MTVR)
1998	H.R. 2266/P.L. 105-56	Section 8008	Apache Longbow radar
			AV-8B aircraft
			Family of Medium Tactical Vehicles
1997	H.R. 3610/P.L. 104-208	Section 8009 of Section 101(b) of Title I of Division A	Javelin missiles
			Army Tactical Missile System (ATACMS)
			Mk19-3 grenade machine guns
			M16A2 rifles
			M249 Squad Automatic Weapons
			M4 carbine rifles
			M240B machine guns
			Arleigh Burke (DDG-15 [sic:51] class destroyers

Fiscal Year	Bill/Law	Section on MYP	Program(s) Approved for MYP
1996	H.R. 2126/P.L. 104-61	Section 8010	UH-60 Blackhawk helicopter
			Apache Longbow helicopter
			M1A2 tank upgrade
1995	H.R. 4650/P.L. 103-335	Section 8010	MK19-3 grenade machine guns
			M16A2 rifles
			M249 Squad Automatic Weapons
			M4 carbine rifles
1994	H.R. 3116/P.L. 103-139	Section 8011	[none]
1993	H.R. 5504/P.L. 102-396	Section 9013[a]	Defense Support Satellites 23, 24 and 25
			Enhanced Modular Signal Processor
1992	H.R. 2521/P.L. 102-172	Section 8013	MK-48 ADCAP Torpedo
			UH-60 Black Hawk helicopter
			Army Tactical missile
1991	H.R. 5803/P.L. 101-511	Section 8014	Line of Sight-Rear (Avenger)—Pedestal Mounted Stinger
			Family of Medium Tactical Vehicles (FMTV)
			LCAC Landing Craft
			LHD Amphibious Ship
			MK-45 Gun Mount/MK-6 Ammo Hoist
			NAVSTAR Global Positioning Satellite (GPS)
			Defense Support Program Satellites 22 and 23
1990	H.R. 3072/P.L. 101-165	Section 9021[a]	M-1 tank engines
			M-1 tank fire control
			Bradley Fighting Vehicle
			Family of Heavy Tactical Vehicles
			Maverick Missile (AGM-65D)
			SH-60B/F helicopter
			DDG-51 destroyer (two years)

Source: Table prepared by CRS based on text of bills.

a. In H.R. 5504/P.L. 102-396 and H.R. 3072/P.L. 101-165, the general provisions title was Title IX.

Author Contact Information

Ronald O'Rourke
Specialist in Naval Affairs
rorourke@crs.loc.gov, 7-7610

Moshe Schwartz
Specialist in Defense Acquisition
mschwartz@crs.loc.gov, 7-1463

www.ingramcontent.com/pod-product-compliance
Lightning Source LLC
Chambersburg PA
CBHW052027280526
45793CB00005B/1160